THEN AND THERE SERIES
GENERAL EDITOR
MARJORIE REEVES

The Elizabethan Country House

MARJORIE REEVES

Illustrated from contemporary sources

LONGMAN

LONGMAN GROUP LIMITED
Longman House, Burnt Mill, Harlow, Essex CM20 2JE, UK
and Associated Companies throughout the World.

First published 1984

ISBN 0 582 20002 4

Set in 12/14pt Baskerville, Linotron 202

Printed in Hong Kong by
Commonwealth Printing Press Ltd

Acknowledgements

We are grateful to the following for permission to reproduce photographs:
BBC Hulton Picture Library, page 44; B.T. Batsford Ltd, page 25; Bodleian Library, Oxford, page 14; British Library, page 48; Country Life, page 31; Fotomas Index, London, page 17; Hardwick Hall, photo: Courtauld Institute of Art, pages 7, National Trust 38 (right), 39; Mansell Collection, pages 8–9, 51, 53, 67; National Trust, cover and pages 4, 13, 26, 33, 35, 36, 37, 38 (left), 63, 65, 69, 70; Victoria and Albert Museum, London, page 27.

2.75

Contents

Hardwick Hall which Bess, the heroine of this book, built between 1591 and 1597. Find the letters 'ES' and coronets. You will see on page 30 what these mean

To the Reader

Is there a big country house anywhere near you which is described as 'Elizabethan'? If so, it will have been built in the time of Queen Elizabeth I who reigned from 1558 to 1603. This book is about a woman of that time who was nicknamed Bess of Hardwick. Her hobby was building or rebuilding houses. But she also spent a lot of time in London and knew many important people.

Queen Elizabeth's father, Henry VIII, had three children and before Elizabeth came to the throne first Edward VI and then Mary had reigned. Edward favoured the new church, called the *Protestant* Church, but Mary belonged to the old *Catholic* Church. When Edward died, some Protestant noblemen tried to make Edward's cousin, Lady Jane Grey, queen instead of Mary, because they knew that Mary would make England go back to the Catholic Church. Their plan failed, Lady Jane was executed and Mary became Queen. So, for a short while, England did indeed return to the Catholic Church. But Mary died after only five years as queen and when Elizabeth succeeded she felt that most English people wanted some sort of Protestant Church of England and so made yet another change back again.

Bess had to live through all these changes. It was dangerous to offend the king or queen. As you will see, she generally managed to keep out of trouble (though not always), and under Queen Elizabeth she became a famous Elizabethan lady.

The value of money has changed a lot since the days of Elizabeth and is changing very fast at present. To turn Elizabethan money into our money today you would probably have to multiply it by about 300. All the figures in this book are given as Elizabethan money.

Words printed in *italics* are explained in the Glossary on page 76.

1 Red-haired Bess

In 1527, when King Henry VIII ruled England, a girl was born into a family of girls at Hardwick in Derbyshire. Perhaps her father, John Hardwick, groaned and said 'Another daughter!' For he was only a country squire and not very well-off and daughters needed *dowries* when they married. But at least this baby girl looked bright: she had red hair and beautiful large eyes. They called her Elizabeth – Bess for short. By the time she was running about, her mother could see that she was sharp-witted and lively and even might be beautiful later on. And she needed to be, for her father died when she was very small and left her only a little more than £20 as a dowry. What was her mother to do with four daughters and a son who was only two years old? She did what was the only possible thing then – married again, to a man who also had three daughters. But they were still quite poor and, anyway, where were the girls going to find husbands living away in Derbyshire, so far from London? So, when she was about twelve, Bess was sent to London to live in the house of a distant cousin, Lady Zouche.

The red-haired girl must have been attractive. The story goes that a young man from Derbyshire, Robert Barley, came to stay at Lady Zouche's and fell ill. Bess helped to nurse him and, as the story says, 'being very

Bess in middle age; this portrait hangs in Hardwick Hall

young and handsome he fell in love with her.' She was about fourteen and he only thirteen years old. It was a child-marriage, but Bess's mother must have been pleased because it brought her daughter a little money. Alas, he died less than two years later and Bess had to fight hard to get the sum of £100 which was due to her.

So before she was grown-up Bess of Hardwick was already a widow and had discovered that you had to fight for your rights and live by your wits. She was now a beautiful young woman, about 1.6 metres tall, very lively and amusing. Because of her hair people later said she was like Queen Elizabeth I. She stayed in London, probably as a lady-in-waiting to a noblewoman and there she met her first real husband, Sir William Cavendish. He fell in love with her beauty and charm. He was forty-two, she was twenty. They were married at the odd time of 2 o'clock in the morning on 20 August 1547. No one knows why the wedding was at this strange time. Can you think of a possible reason?

After this Bess's life was much more comfortable. She didn't have to worry about money because Cavendish, though not a nobleman, was a gentleman with a fair income, and a country house in Hertfordshire and a town house in London. He also had a job at the Court. Bess was fond of her husband and perhaps still more fond of being mistress in her own house. She had about fifteen

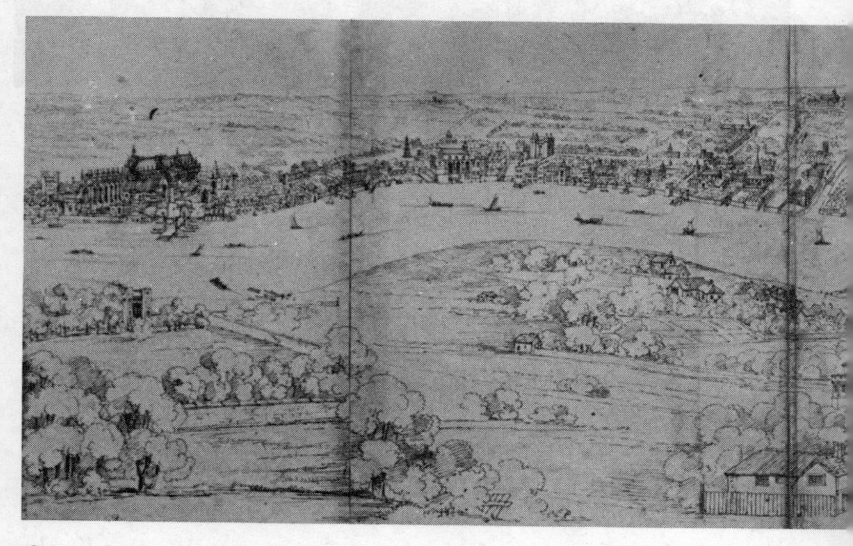

Sixteenth-century London drawn by Anthony van Wyngaerde in about 1543. Find St Paul's (with a spire) and London Bridge (with shops on it)

servants and a 'gentlewoman' named Cecily to wait on her.

Bess's husband taught her to keep accounts and from these we can find out quite a lot about how the Cavendishes lived in their London house down by the river. They liked to give parties in their *parlour* and, as their grand guests brought plenty of servants with them, there would be a second dinner party going on in the hall. Their own servants wore blue *livery* and, of course, waited on them at home and when they went visiting.

Dinner was at the strange time of 11 a.m. and supper at 6 p.m. No one seemed to eat much breakfast. Bess liked decorating her parlour with green branches and flowers when she was having a party. They kept a harpist and a *minstrel* to sing and play while they ate enormous

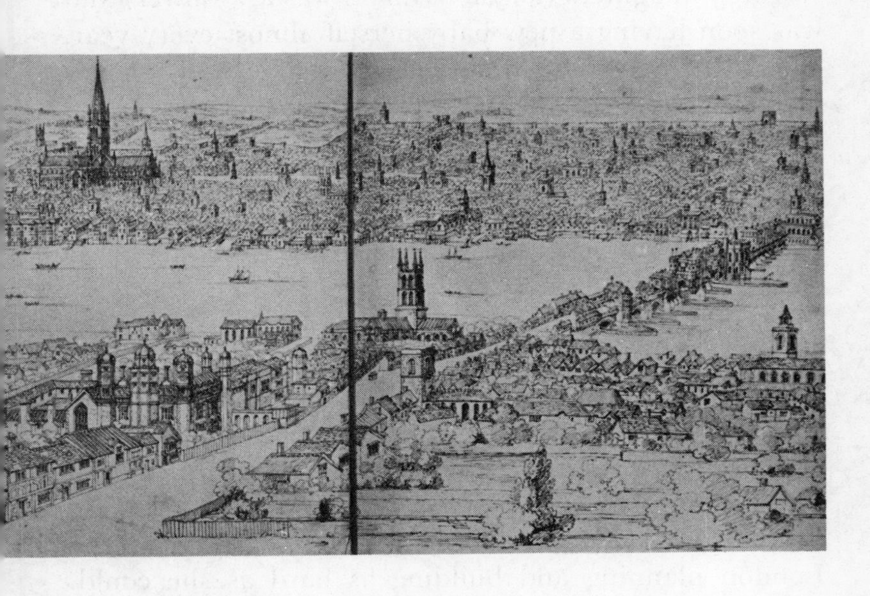

dinners or suppers with their friends. Here are some of the things which we find from the accounts that they ate: fresh salmon boiled in ale; crabs and oysters; all the usual joints of lamb, veal and beef; ox's feet; blackbirds; 'a dish of 12 great birds and 12 dozen small birds'. They went in for lots of salads, and spices like cinnamon, ginger and cloves, and they could get fruit like dates, raisins, figs, oranges and almonds.

When they went out to parties they could take a boat up the river or Bess could go in her splendid new *litter* which was lined with green quilted silk. They really lived a very pleasant life and spent a good deal of money. Their household expenses came to something like £40 a week, over £10,000 in our money today.

Bess was soon busy with her family. She started with two step-daughters (for Sir William was a widower) and was soon having a new baby herself almost every year. Altogether she had 8 children, but only 6 lived to grow up: 3 sons and 3 daughters. It was more dangerous for women to have children then and we find Bess and her husband in 1549 paying the midwife what was then quite a large sum of 50s. (£2.50). But Bess was a healthy young woman and she managed to have all these children and do many other things as well.

At this time Bess and her husband were buying a larger house and a lot of land at Chatsworth up in Derbyshire. They bought the old Chatsworth house for £600 in 1549. Bess was thrilled. She had all kinds of schemes for building a grander house and furnishing it with beautiful things. For the next few years she went backwards and forwards between Derbyshire and London planning and building as hard as she could.

Bess and her husband loved each other, but Sir

William had to spend much time at Court on his job. When Bess was at Chatsworth he wrote loving letters calling her 'my own sweet Bess' or 'My own, more dear than I am to myself'. Once he sent a whole basket of things to her by a servant. It contained artichokes, cucumbers, Spanish silk for her embroidery, wire to mend her *virginals*, olives and *sturgeon*. Bess must have enjoyed unpacking it. Even when he got leave to go to Chatsworth he was sometimes called back on the way, but when he and his 9 servants and 10 horses finally clattered up to the door, how glad they must have been and how eager he would be to see all the new building work at Chatsworth.

2 Bringing up Children

Like many Elizabethan ladies Bess took great care over bring up her children properly. She had nursemaids to look after them when they were little but used to see them very often. Here is a little scene written at that time in which a lady visits her baby in the nursery – you can imagine it is Bess talking:

LADY: *Good morrow*, Nurse.
NURSE: God give you good morrow, Madame.
LADY: How *doth* the child?
NURSE: He is fair and plump and does very well, thanks be to God.
LADY: Undo his *swaddling bands*. Have you clean water to wash him? Oh, my little heart! God bless thee. Rub the crown of his head, wash his ears and his face. *Hath* he not a pimple upon his nose? His little cheeks are wet, I believe you did leave him alone to cry. How many teeth has he? Thou art pretty and fat, my little darling. His thumb is flea-bitten, are there any fleas in your *chamber*? [After the washing is finished] Where is his little petticoat? Give him his coat of *changeable taffeta* and his satin sleeves. Where is his bib? Let him have his gathered apron with strings and hang a *muckinder* to it.... Now put him in his cradle and rock him till he sleeps but first let me kiss him. God send thee good

rest, my little boykin. I pray you, good Nurse, have a care of him.

NURSE: Do not doubt it, Madame, with the grace of God.

As you can guess from that baby's clothes, Elizabethan children were dressed like little grown-ups. When Frances, Bess's first child, was a year old she was put into petticoats made of wool and a bodice, with a waistcoat on top. She also had a red cloak and she was given a teething-ring. This picture shows you how children were dressed. It is a picture of Bess's grand-daughter, Arabella Stuart (see pages 66–8), who is dressed rather grandly because some people thought she might one day become queen of England and Scotland.

When she had been to London Bess brought the children wooden dolls with painted faces, (look at the one Arabella is holding in the picture) toy soldiers, drums and hoops, balls and spinning tops. And they played many games like ours, such as blind man's buff, leap-frog and skittles.

Soon there were lessons to learn. The children began with a *horn-book* which looked like this:

The paper was fixed on a board and covered with horn to protect it. (What would be used today instead of horn?) If you look at it carefully you will see how much a child could learn from it. Because of the cross at the top the first alphabet row was called the criss-cross row. After the horn-book the children went on to simple reading books. They carefully copied out sentences in their best hand-writing in copy-books. Then they got on to arithmetic and grammar. They had to learn to cut their own pens from a *quill* feather with a sharp pen-knife.

Bess's children did their lessons at home and were taught by *tutors*. As they grew older they had long school hours. They got up about 6.30 a.m., went to prayers with the whole household, or said prayers with the tutor, and had a bite for breakfast. Lessons began at 8 o'clock with an hour learning French and Latin. From 9 to 10 they had dancing or music lessons and then some exercise. At 10 a.m. they settled down to writing, arithmetic, or perhaps drawing, and a Bible lesson. How they must have looked forward to dinner at 11! They had two hours off then and time to play. At 1 o'clock they were back in their schoolroom to do cosmography (geography), then French and Latin again between 2 and 3 p.m., then more writing and grammar, and finally prayers again before their supper at 6 p.m. After all that, they really had earned some time for play.

What do you think of that for a school day? Count up how many hours they were actually doing lessons. What lessons do you have which these children did not get? Maybe some were dull, but cosmography was exciting because it was about the new parts of the world which adventurous sailors were discovering at that time.

Perhaps the children looked at one of the new maps showing strange places which people in England had never dreamed of before. If you got a parcel from your father in London which contained three French grammars and a geography book you might be a bit disappointed, as the Cavendish children must have been when they got it. But then a pedlar came round with little story-books called chapbooks and their mother bought them tales of King Arthur and of the giant, Guy of Warwick. So they had some exciting stories as well.

The children enjoyed music and dancing. You will read about some of the dances they learned later on. Music was very important, for at a party everyone was expected to be able to sing in a *madrigal* or a *catch* and to play on the *lute* or *recorder*. The boys did get some sports training as well. They learned to wrestle with each other and to fence, that is, to have a mock fight with thin swords, called *rapiers*. And they played football and a kind of tennis.

Bess and her husband were strict with their children. They slept on hard beds and had simple food and mostly water to drink. Their breakfast would be bread and butter and fruit. For dinner they would have a thick soup called pottage, made of vegetables and bits of meat, with a salad to go with it. Supper would be bread and butter and fruit again. At table each child would have a trencher (a piece of bread for a plate), a drinking mug and spoon. They used their fingers instead of forks. At the end of the meal they were taught to clean their knives and put them back in their sheaths, and to wash their face and hands, using a jug and basin of water. If their parents were there they knelt down and asked for their blessing.

Children playing games after their lessons are over. How many different games can you see?

Grown-ups thought good manners were very important, so the children were taught to stand up when their elders came into the room and to keep quiet when grown-ups were talking. The boys learnt how to bow and how to *doff* their caps to people. The girls had to practise curtseying. They were even taught how to blow their noses. Do you think it is a good idea to learn manners like that?

Here is another little scene written at the time in which a lady, who might be Bess, visits the boys and their master.

LADY: Good morrow, Master, I am glad to find your scholars so well employed at their books, as I see you do not keep them idle. You know that they are put in your charge not only to teach them grammar and Latin, but also good manners and their duties. Have you said your prayers this morning, boys?

BOYS: Yes, Mother, so soon as we are risen and have put on our clothes and washed.

LADY: Go to, read me this chapter. [The boys read.] It is not enough to read. Those that be wise read for their understanding and not for the sound of words only. You are past your A.B.C. that we give to little children to learn to sound the words. You must be better than parrots. Now which of you writes best?

WILLIAM: It is my brother Henry.

LADY: Hold then, Henry, there is a *gilded ink-horn* that I give you to encourage you to learn the better.

HENRY: I must humbly thank you, Mother, truly it is fair.

LADY: William, what do you think of your brother's ink-horn? If I thought you would envy him, I would have you soundly whipped, for there is nothing so absurd or blockish as envy.

MASTER: But Madame, I had forgotten to tell you that your son Henry is slow to rise in the morning, for one must call him three or four times before he comes out of his bed.

LADY: You can cure that with the juice of the *birch*, if you will apply it only twice or thrice. And if that medicine will not work, I will give him such a morning song that he will leap out of bed. Now boys, do you wear your clothes like gentlemen? Put on your silver-embroidered garters, for you shall go out with me. Have you clean handkerchers? Button your *doublets* and brush your breeches. Take your cloaks lined with taffeta and your rapiers with silver hilts.

What do you think the Lady meant by the 'juice of the birch'?

As you can see, fathers and mothers could be very strict. When the Cavendish boys were naughty their father or their tutor would whip them really hard with that nasty little birch made of twigs which stung so much. But Henry and William must have wished themselves back at home when, aged ten and nine, they were sent to the famous school at Eton for a year. The boys had a ten-hour school day and only one afternoon a week off. They had about sixteen days holiday at Christmas and twelve at Easter. A man-servant went with them and kept an account of what he spent on shows, clothes and small things. They cost £25 for the year. Once he wrote down '3d. to see the *bear-baiting* and the camel', so they did have some fun sometimes, and acting Latin plays at school made a change for them. But the boys must have been glad to get home again.

When he was fifteen William went to Clare College, Cambridge, where he learnt a great many things, including geometry, *astronomy*, mathematics, Greek and Hebrew. So, whether he liked it or not, he was well educated!

When Henry, Bess's eldest son, was twenty-one he went travelling round Europe on what was called the Grand Tour. This meant that with a tutor and several servants he rolled around in a large coach, or sometimes rode on horseback, to many famous places to see the sights and do some study. Like other young Englishmen of that time, he particularly wanted to go to Italy where there were famous artists and architects and therefore many splendid pictures, sculptures and buildings to see.

What about the girls? They also learnt many things, but they stayed at home. They had a mistress to themselves and some special visiting masters for subjects like French and dancing. Here again is a short dialogue in which you can imagine Bess talking to her daughters and their mistress, Clemence:

[The maidservant comes to call them]

MAID: Up! My Lady is already in the gallery and bids you come and bring your work with you.

CLEMENCE: Did I not tell you so? It grieves me very much to see you so *sluggish*. I have called you an hour before you began to rise.

FRANCES: I pray you do not tell our mother and we will be more *diligent* in future. Sister, where is our needlework? I have forgotten my needlecase. Wait a little, I have not my silver thimble.

[They greet their mother in the gallery]

LADY: Frances, is this your *cut-work*? I see a fault in it but the edge is reasonably well made. Mary, are your tapestry cushions done?

MARY: I have only one cushion to do and I lack silk, for all my gold and silver thread is done.

LADY: Mistress Clemence, let them have what they need, so that they lose no time. At what hours do your masters come?

FRANCES: Our dancing master comes about nine o'clock; our singing master and he that teaches us to play on the virginals at ten; he that teaches us to play the lute and the *viola da gamba* at four in the afternoon. Our French master comes between seven and eight in the morning.

LADY: Now go in God's name, whom I pray to fill you with his grace.

Already, when her daughters were small Bess was busy planning for them to marry noblemen with large houses and many servants. So she had to teach them to be good at managing a big household, as she was herself. She knew that servants would obey mistresses who could do many household jobs themselves, so she taught her daughters to spin and weave cloth, to cook, to make butter and cheese and to brew medicines from herbs, as well as doing beautiful embroidery and playing musical instruments elegantly.

Several people wrote books of advice on what girls ought to know. For instance, there was 'The Good Housewives' Closet of Provisions' which said that they should be able to make confections [sweets] and *conserves* [jam], decorate gingerbread and marchpane [marzipan], and distil vinegar of roses. They had to know how to carve a joint of meat, keep a good eye on the butler and the *Yeoman* of the Cellar, and organise the dairy. Then they had to know all the plants in the herb garden and which illnesses you could cure with the medicines you made. They even learnt to make perfumes from violets, roses and lavender, and also cosmetics. Their needlework lessons began with learning to embroider a *sampler*, that is, doing alphabets, numbers and sometimes little verses on canvas in various stitches, like cross-stitch and tent-stitch.

3 Building Country Houses

In the reign of Queen Elizabeth many rich people were building beautiful new houses in different parts of England. They no longer had to have houses like fortresses to guard against attacking enemies. Instead of little slits of windows to shoot from, you could have big glass windows and enjoy the view. Instead of *moats* full of water for protection, you could have gardens to walk in.

Elizabethan ladies and gentlemen liked living in the country as well as going to the Queen's court. They liked making elaborate gardens, raising herds of cattle or deer in their parks, hunting, fishing and other country sports. They built their country houses on a definite plan (not like the old houses which were often a muddle, with bits stuck on here and there) and quite often they were shaped like an E or an H. They wanted to live grandly, so inside the main rooms were large, the main staircase was wide and often richly decorated and there was often a long gallery on the first or second floor where people could stroll on a wet day – or even ride their horses! Fireplaces with chimneys were a fairly new luxury so they built lots of chimney stacks with fancy decorations.

As soon as they had bought Chatsworth Sir William and Bess began planning a completely new house. A mason named Roger Word made them a plan for the new house at the cost of £1. Nowadays a wealthy person employs a building contractor to hire workers and carry out the plan but in those days you had to arrange all this yourself. Since Sir William had to be in London a good deal, it was Bess who stayed at Chatsworth and directed the work. She was soon busy giving orders for cutting down trees, buying and carting stone, getting Derby marble for carving figures, and laying in limestone and coal for making plaster.

Then she had to find a whole army of building workers. There were usually about thirty on the job and once – in the summer – about eighty. She needed stonemasons and slaters, plasterers and glaziers, sawyers, carpenters and wood-carvers. The carvers had to be skilled to make the wooden panelling for the walls of the best rooms. They decorated it with bits of different coloured wood inlaid (inserted) in the panels to make patterns. Stonemasons carved elaborate *overmantels* in *alabaster* with figures like this of the Greek god Apollo and the Muses.

Then the gardens had to be laid out. The orchard, usually on one side of the house, had all kinds of fruit trees: apple, plum, pear, mulberry, *quince*, apricot, *medlar*, as well as nut trees. It was a pleasant place for strolling on a hot day. On the side of the house was the vegetable garden. One part would be a special herb garden of plants like sage, thyme, mint, fennel and many more, all used for flavouring food or for medicines. You would have been surprised to see cowslips, primroses, violets and marigolds in the vegetable garden, but the Elizabethans used them in salads. They grew sweet-scented flowers and herbs to make posies that would drown the smells from *privies* and drains.

In front of the house Elizabethans made flower gardens. This was an exciting new idea. They were usually very formal, that is, with a definite pattern of paths and flower beds. First we should walk out on to a gravelled terrace overlooking the garden and the park and then down fine flights of steps into a pattern of flower beds edged with little clipped hedges. Elizabethans called this a *knot-garden*; the pattern might look like the one on the opposite page.

Sometimes they made a maze of little paths and hedges through which people would search to find the centre. In summer time the flower beds would be bright with pinks and peonies, sweet williams and pansies, poppies, larkspur, crown imperials, lilies and many more flowers.

You may be wondering why there is no photograph of Bess's beautiful new Chatsworth in this book. The reason is that after Bess's time the Cavendish family had even grander ideas. So they pulled down the Elizabethan house and built a more splendid one which you can see

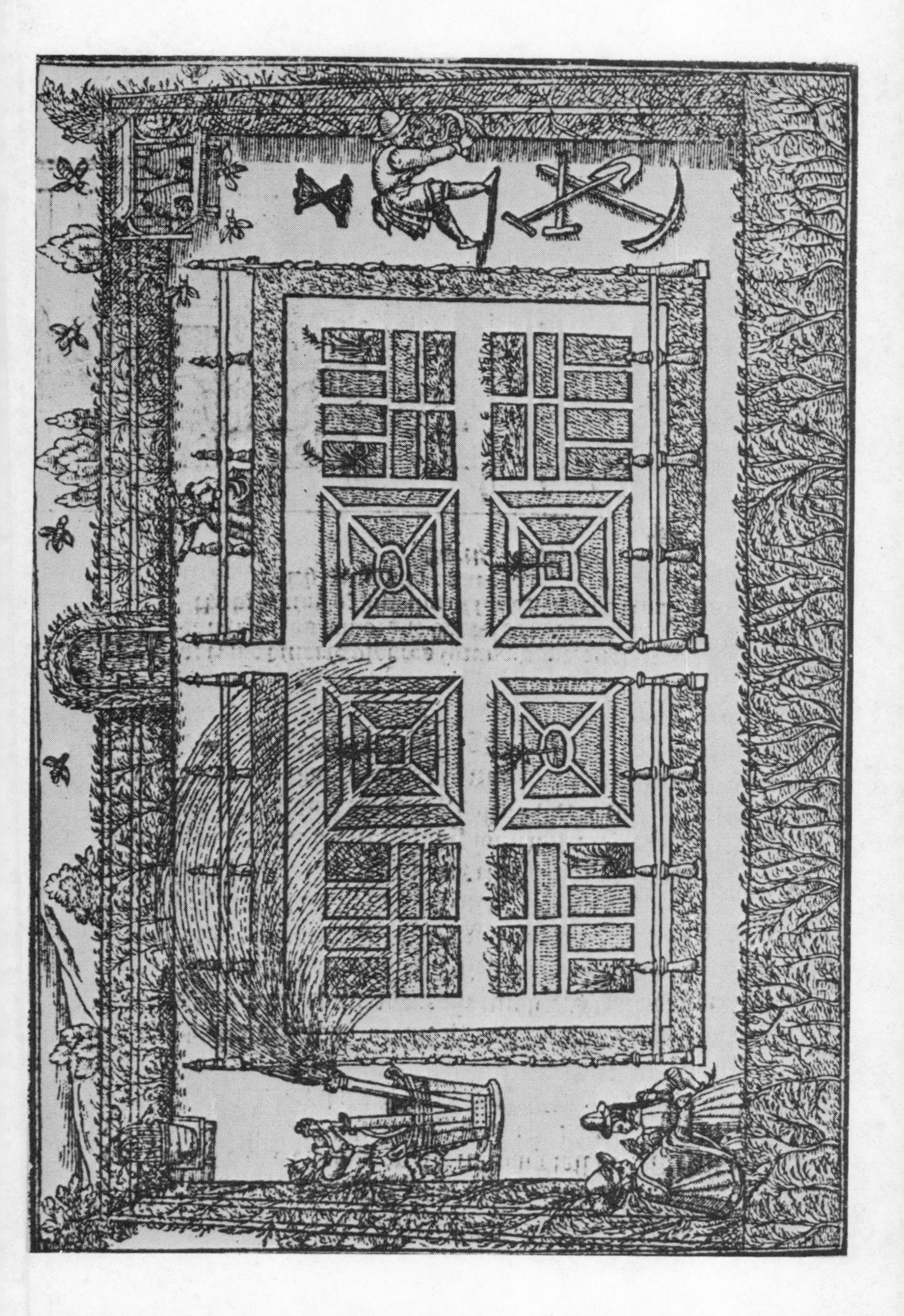

today if you visit Derbyshire. But luckily for us Bess or one of her ladies did this needlework picture of her Chatsworth.

We can imagine what Chatsworth was like inside from reading Bess's building accounts. We should have gone in through that central archway into a courtyard with buildings all round. On the opposite side of the courtyard we would go through a porch into the great hall. At one end of this was the grand staircase leading right up to the second floor where the most magnificent rooms, the gallery and Great High Chamber, were. The family rooms were on the first floor.

Bess's accounts tell us that on the walls of the best rooms she hung forty-two *tapestries* picturing old Greek stories of battles and also hunting scenes, all woven in rich colours of red, purple, gold and blue. Tapestries were beautiful to look at but they also helped to keep the draughts out. Bess and her husband slept in a big gilded bedstead with red curtains round it and a red and silver *valance*, with a quilt of red *sarsenet* to match. Later, when Bess had an *inventory* made, we find that there were thirteen bedchambers at Chatsworth, each with carved and gilded beds and matching curtains, coverlets and cushions (see page 72 to read a piece from Bess's inventory about her best bedchamber). Beds like the one below were the most expensive things in the rooms. Notice the panelled walls and decorated plaster ceiling. The rest of the furniture would be chests, tables and stools, with matting or just rushes on the floor.

But before the house was finished Sir William Cavendish was dead. Bess and he had been really fond of each other and when he died she wrote in a notebook: 'Mem. that Sir William Cavendish, Knight, my most dear and well-beloved husband departed this present life on Monday. On whose soul I most humbly beseech [ask] the Lord to have mercy and to rid me and his poor children out of our great misery'.

Sir William had died owing £5,000 to the Crown, so Bess was again in trouble about money and she had six children to bring up. She did what was at the time the most sensible thing to do and found another husband at Court – Sir William St Loe. In spite of her debts he fell in love with her and they were married in 1561 and were very happy. When he was at Court and she at Chatsworth he wrote to her often addressing her rather quaintly as 'My honest, sweet Chatsworth' or 'My own good servant and chief *overseer*' or 'My own, more dear to me than I am to myself'. When she did not write he was anxious, so he wrote: 'As thou dost love me, let me shortly hear from thee for the quieting of my unquieted mind, how thine own sweet self doth. Thus wishing myself with thyself, I bid thee most heartily farewell'. You can see a picture of Bess when she was Lady St Loe on page 7.

But once again Bess lost her husband who died in 1564, and once again she came back to Court to find another – her fourth husband. This time she did even better for herself by marrying George Talbot, the sixth Earl of Shrewsbury. So she became the Countess of Shrewsbury. He, like her previous husbands, had to spend much time away from her and at first he wrote most lovingly. His nickname for her was 'sweet none', which probably means 'my own'. Once, when he got a letter from her after a long gap he replied saying that he was just about to send a servant to find out how she was, since he had not heard for so long and this drove him into the dumps. But now, he says, he is happy: 'I thank you, sweet none, for your puddings and *venison*. God send me soon home to possess my greatest joy: if you think it is you, you are not deceived'.

George Talbot was a widower with children of his own, so he and Bess arranged marriages between their children. Gilbert Talbot, who later became the seventh Earl, married Bess's daughter Mary, and Bess's eldest son, Henry, married Grace Talbot. They might have had a happy family circle of Cavendishes and Talbots, but later on – we don't really know why – Bess and her husband quarrelled violently. Once, when Bess had flounced off in a rage, Gilbert, her step-son, tried to make peace between them, telling his father: 'My lord, when she [Bess] told me of her dear love towards you and how your lordship had paid her, she was in such a *perplexity*, as I never saw woman'. To this the Earl replied: 'I know her love hath been great to me and mine hath been and is as great to her, what could a man do more for his wife than I have done?' By this time Gilbert had a little son, George, so he tried to get Bess back by writing to her about her grandson:

> George is very well. I thank God he drinketh every day to Lady Grandmother and if he has any spice [not good for children] I tell him Lady grandmother is coming and will see him. Then he will either quickly eat or quickly hide it and than ask 'Where is Lady Danmode?'

But the quarrel between husband and wife got worse and in the end Bess went back to her old home at Hardwick. She had now bought this and so, once again, she started doing what she most liked – building a new house.

4 Bess's Hardwick

Bess's new house at Hardwick is not difficult to imagine, like Chatsworth, because it is still there. You might be able to visit it one day. At first Bess lived in the old house, adding a new storey on top. But soon she found the old house uncomfortable and was making plans for the new one.

Building started in 1591. The plan of Bess's new house was shaped like a double cross. This was a new idea, and there was no other house like it then. If we look at the picture on page 4 we see the west front of the house very much as Bess saw it. Perhaps the first things that catch our eye are the *turrets* on the roof decorated round the top with stone *coronets* and the initials ES (for Elizabeth Shrewsbury). Bess meant everyone who came to know who she was. Next we notice what a great number of windows there are and how the windows get bigger as we look upwards. 'Hardwick Hall, more glass than wall', someone said.

You can guess how busy Bess and her chief servants were, finding all the workers and building materials. John the Painter was the main overseer. She paid him £2 a year and gave him a farm. Labourers cut down trees in the park for floors and beams, quarried and carted stone and dug out the foundations and cellars in four weeks. Then came the stonemasons to build and after them glaziers had to be found to put in the big glass windows. Peter Yates, a carpenter, put the roof on for £50. After that John the Painter got busy decorating the rooms and Bess's accounts show her buying vermilion, white lead, lamp black, yellow ochre, gold and gum for him. Abraham Smith made elaborate overmantels in plaster work and Thomas Accres carved some beautiful alabaster overmantels. He also invented a machine for cutting stone which pleased Bess so much that she gave his wife 40*s.* (£2) to buy a gown.

While all this was going on Bess made a long visit to London. She travelled there slowly in a huge coach with no springs, drawn by six horses with ES on their silver harness. Ahead of her she had sent furniture for her London house as well as forty sheep and two fat oxen to feed her household, for she took about forty servants with her. The journey to London took seven days. As her coach and procession of riders trotted through the towns

A country coach embroidered perhaps by Bess for a chair in the High Great Chamber. When going to London, Bess's coach was grander

people would run to ring the church bells and turn out to stare at the grand lady.

The first thing Bess did in London was to buy a lot of new clothes. She spent more than £300 on dresses, perfumed gloves and Spanish leather shoes. She attended Court for a great Christmas party, went to *banquets* and *masques*, and later sailed down the river for dancing at the royal palace at Greenwich. But she had also come to London to buy things for her new house – gold and silver dishes and goblets (costing £1,200) and tapestries. She also bought a splendid new litter upholstered in *tawny* velvet. When she finally set out for home she travelled in the new litter and behind her came nine waggons with all she had bought and forty-three servants on horse-back. What a spree she must have had!

After she got back to Hardwick building work started again. The privies had to be built in the courtyard; there were, of course, no bathrooms. At last the house was furnished and Bess moved in with her grand-daughter, Arabella Stuart, who was then living with her.

We can take a look at her house for ourselves. When we visit Hardwick we shall not find the rooms looking exactly as Bess left them: some furniture has been moved or lost; some was made much later. But we do know what Bess had in each room because she made an inventory in 1601 in which everything was listed. On pages 72–3 you can read a bit of this.

We go into the hall through a pillared entrance (or screen). It would have been brighter in Bess's time because of the brilliant tapestries on the walls, which were probably hunting scenes. Over the fireplace are the Hardwick coat of arms and the two Hardwick stags, with the countess's coronet above (see page 70). The hall is 29

The Great Hall, Hardwick. The screen has embroideries of famous Greek. people like Penelope. Notice the tapestries on the wall

metres long and at the far end we can see another screen of splendid embroidery, probably made by Bess's women from pieces of velvet, silk and cloth of gold. In Bess's time there were three long tables in the hall with benches to sit on and probably there were 'cup-boards' against the walls. These were shelves for showing off your beautiful cups and goblets. (This is how we get our word 'cupboard'.) On either side of the hall were the kitchens, *buttery* and pantry.

The newest fashion in Bess's time was for the master or mistress to live mostly on the first floor and to this Bess added an idea of her own. (She had done the same at Chatsworth and at the old house at Hardwick.) This was to build a second floor and put the grandest rooms with the largest windows up there for her important guests. So from the hall we go up the main staircase with wide, shallow steps and, as we go, we can picture grand ladies in enormous *farthingales* sweeping up.

On the first floor we stop outside Bess's *withdrawing room*. In this room, in Bess's day, there was a black leather chair with gilded patterns which was probably hers, and a little chair covered in cloth of gold, with a gold and red silk fringe which was probably for her grand-daughter, Arabella. For any visiting grand-children there were two small chairs and lots of embroidered stools. We should admire the long cushions of gold and red *damask* and crimson velvet and the tapestries covering the walls. Perhaps we might want to look inside the great iron-bound chest in which Bess kept her money.

Sad to say, when we get into Bess's bedchamber we shall not see her bed. It must have been a gorgeous one, for the head, the *tester* and posts were covered in scarlet with silver lace laid on and it had scarlet and silver curtains and a valance embroidered with gold thistles. She had six Spanish blankets and two quilts and somewhere in the room there were five purple curtains. She had a chair of *russet* satin striped with silver, a table with a *turkey carpet* on it, some stools, several trunks and more embroidered cushions. What do you miss in that bedroom? Arabella slept in a little room opening out of her grandmother's. Her bed was hung with yellow and blue satin embroidered with gold flowers.

From her bedchamber Bess would go across through the gallery above the end of the hall to what she called the Low Great Chamber which was her dining-room. In those days the walls were hung with eight tapestries and there was a long carved inlaid table for meals, which was covered with a turkey carpet, and some gorgeous chairs and stools. One chair was covered with cloth of gold and silver, with green velvet patterns laid on top and a green silk fringe. And there were cushions galore – gold, silver, crimson with silver spangles and gold tassels, silver and green with a raised rose embroidered in the middle, and so on. The room must have glowed with colour.

Climbing the stairs again we come into the High Great Chamber and marvel at its height and size and huge windows on one side. It is 20 metres long, 10 metres wide and 26 metres high. Bess must have received many grand ladies and gentlemen and there would be room for a great number, even with their stuffed-out clothes! The

The High Great Chamber, Hardwick. The frieze shows Diana and many different animals

The Long Gallery, Hardwick

plaster frieze round the walls shows the goddess Diana in the midst of many animals such as deer, lions and elephants, all feeding peacefully together. Bess chose Diana as a compliment to Queen Elizabeth who was often called Diana. She hoped the Queen would visit Hardwick one day and would be pleased to see herself as a goddess of peace and happiness.

Beyond the Great High Chamber is the Withdrawing Room and beyond this room was the best bedchamber, but we will now go into the Long Gallery. As you can see from the picture opposite, it is magnificent.

It is 50 metres long, running the whole length of the house, with large windows, including two bays, all along one side. On the wall opposite are thirteen tapestries. In Bess's time there was not much furniture in the gallery: two inlaid tables, three chairs, some stools, and embroidered cushions on the window seats. On page 72 you can read a piece of the inventory about the gallery. Today you will see here embroidered chairs, called farthingale chairs, which look like this one. Ladies with large

Bess in later life, wearing a widow's cap

Sir William Cavendish

farthingales found ordinary chairs difficult to sit on but they would lean against this kind. These chairs were actually made later than Bess's time but she probably had some like them.

One reason for having a gallery was to hang pictures. So as we walk along it we can see some of Bess's pictures (as well as some painted later). You can see a picture of Bess herself on page 7. Now here she is with three of her husbands.

Then there are several of her children and two of her grand-daughter Arabella, one when a baby (see page 13) and one of her as a young woman.

There are famous people whom Bess knew and – most important – the picture of Queen Elizabeth which you see on page 40 and one of Mary Queen of Scots (see page

Sir William St Loe. Why was he called Bess's third husband?

George Talbot, Earl of Shrewsbury

63). Perhaps when Bess was an old lady she would go slowly along the gallery looking at all those faces and remembering the many people in her life.

We can see more rooms at Hardwick, some grand, some not so grand. As we walk round two things strike us particularly. One is how proud Bess was of her families. Wherever possible – on overmantels, on tapestries, embroidered on cushions, inlaid on tables – the coats of arms, crests and badges of Hardwick, Cavendish and Talbot are pictured. If you visit Hardwick, see how many you can find. Secondly, we notice many fine embroideries, done by Bess or her women and also, as you will read later, by Bess and Mary Queen of Scots. Most of these embroideries are now framed behind glass but they were first done for cushions or chairs, or in

Portrait of Queen Elizabeth I at Hardwick, about 1595

strips for bed-curtains, coverlets or wall-hangings. Bess embroidered flowers and fruits with gold and silver thread on velvet, and even put in caterpillars and snails.

Bess's house must have been full of colour: blues, scarlets, purples, greens and gold. It was all very splendid, but I wonder how comfortable it was to live in?

5 *Living in a Country House*

Living in a big Elizabethan house meant much ceremonial, that is, elaborate ways of doing things. The master and mistress lived grandly, but this meant much hard work for the servants. Bess and her husband had ladies and gentlemen of the bedchamber to wake them in the morning. Bess's ladies would get up early, make sure that they had cleaned their teeth and finger nails and then warm their mistress's clothes and fill the wooden bath tub in front of the fire with warm, scented water. They had balls of sweet-scented soap, home-made from almonds and *musk* or rose-leaves and lavender. Bess cleaned her teeth with tooth soap and a linen cloth (no tooth brush). The waiting lady would comb her hair with an ivory comb, perhaps forty times, as one writer advised, and then it was the page's turn to clean the comb.

Dressing was quite a business, for as Bess grew older fashionable clothes for both men and women grew more and more elaborate. Look at the clothes worn by Bess on page 7, by Arabella on page 67, and by Elizabeth on page 40. Bess first put on an embroidered *chemise* and a bright-coloured petticoat. Over the chemise went a *bodice* stiffened with whale-bone stays. Under the petticoat was fastened the farthingale to make her skirts stick out; this was made of wire hoops or sometimes a roll stiffened with wire. Next she put on a kirtle which was a dress in two parts, bodice and skirt, open at top and bottom. A stomacher, which was a piece of rich material stiffened with cardboard, was pushed into the top gap and another piece went into the bottom gap. On top of all this Bess's maid would put a loose gown, open in front to show the bright colours underneath. Kirtle and gown were made of expensive stuffs, such as velvet, taffeta and cloth of gold or silver, often embroidered or decorated with ribbons. Scarlet, blue, yellow and tawny were favourite colours and some of Bess's gowns had elaborate separate sleeves in contrasting colours with long hanging ends which, said one scornful writer, had to be slung over the shoulder 'like cows' tails'. Bess's huge *ruff* or stiff upstanding collar was often decorated with gold or silver lace or spangled with sun, moon and stars. Her silk *hose* were of all sorts of colours and her embroidered slippers too.

Bess, like other ladies, went in for elaborate hair-dos. Her maids curled and frizzed and crisped her hair and propped it up with wires. Sometimes Bess wore a wreath of gold and silver or perhaps she hung ornaments in her hair. And right on top of what the scornful writer called 'these stately turrets of hair' her maid would perch a little hat of velvet or taffeta. It was fashionable to have a very red and white make-up. So Bess would bleach her skin and then put on vermilion make-up. She was careful to wash her face in rose-water because the bleaching powder could spoil your skin. Finally, if Bess was dressing for company, she would have her hair perfumed, put on a lot of jewellery, take a pair of fine scented gloves and hang a little mirror and a *pomander* from the velvet girdle round her waist. When she was ready she really was a splendid sight.

Elizabeth noblemen, like their wives, also liked to dress up. You can read about their clothes in another Then and There book called 'The Elizabethan Court'. They loved bright colours and gave them names like popingay blue, drake's satin, lady blush satin, marigold taffeta, lusty gallant and devil in the hedge – what colours do you think those last two were?

Once dressed and having eaten a light breakfast, Bess would go round the great house, for a lady had to train her servants and keep a sharp eye on them. She had quite an army of servants but each knew exactly what his or her job was and everything was done in an orderly way. In the great kitchen fires would be roaring away with huge stew pots bubbling over and red-faced boys called turnspits turning the dripping roasts. We should see the baker pulling *manchet* loaves out of the big brick oven and at the great wooden tables cooks would be chopping up all kinds of joints or preparing poultry or game. There were other rooms for special work: the pastry with two ovens for making pastry, a buttery for drinks, a *spicery*, a brew-house, a pantry and a *servery*. In each of these servants would be bustling round when Bess came to inspect.

Many things which we now buy were made at home, so we should see servants pickling, smoking and salting meat, bacon and fish in great wooden tubs. It was a rule that when visitors or strangers arrived they must be fed, whether they were rich or poor. So they had to keep huge stocks of food, and remember, they had no deep freeze. In the distillery we should find them making wine – cowslip, elderberry, or cider according to season and also mead from honey. We should see the ale brewing too. Some maids would be candying fruit and flowers to make

Kitchen scene. What are the three women doing? What is the cat doing? Find the spit for roasting

sweet syrups and jellies, while the dairymaids would be busy making butter and cheese. From the herb garden girls would be bringing in parsley, thyme, mint, garlic and other herbs to hang up in bundles for drying. All the cooking fat was saved to make candles and soap and in the distillery girls made perfumes of lavender, rosemary, roses and pinks, or washes for their complexions from many different flowers. The laundry women would be beating the linen with wooden bats (for they had no detergents) and then spreading it on the grass to bleach. If they killed a goose the sewing girls used the feathers for making a new feather bed.

The biggest meal in the day was dinner at about 11 a.m. There was a huge menu for dinner. At big feasts there would be about sixteen dishes in the first course and fourteen in the second. Even on ordinary days many dishes would be served. People chose what they wanted and there was usually a lot left over, first for the army of servants and then for all the poor who came to the kitchen knowing that they would be fed. Often there would be workmen like carpenters and blacksmiths to feed, or carters who had brought loads of oats and provisions, and in harvest time the kitchen might cook a whole ox to send out to hungry harvesters in the fields. One Elizabethan writer said that a good lord loved three things: an open cellar, a full hall and a sweating cook, and that he always provided three dinners: one for himself, his family and guests, one for his servants and one for the poor.

Dinner was a solemn affair. The Yeoman of the *Ewry* got ready silver jugs and basins of scented rosewater for hand-washing. The Yeoman of the Cellar bowed to the high table and brought out the wine and goblets for drinking. For the chief people these would be of silver or crystal or Venetian glass shining purple or blue. The Yeoman of the Pantry appeared and bowed to the table. Then the Gentleman *Usher* announced to the lord and lady that dinner was ready. The servants would march in in two processions, one from the kitchen and one from the pantry, carrying all the food on large dishes. They were led by the Usher carrying his rod who called out: 'Speak softly, my masters!' Then all the servants stood in the great hall while the food was placed on the *buffets* and the carver did his work.

Like many Elizabethans, Bess would dine in her own rooms on the first floor, with her ladies and gentlemen. So their dishes were carried upstairs and then all the other servants sat down at the long tables in the hall. There would be about forty in all. They sat in strict order of rank. There was one table for the clerks of the kitchen, the master cook, the usher and other head servants. At another sat the barber, the footmen, *falconers*, grooms, and the birdcatcher. Lower down were the laundry maids and porters. Lowest of all were the scullery maids and kitchen boys. At table everyone had in front of them a squared slice of bread as a trencher, a spoon and a pewter mug. They used their own knives but had no forks for these were hardly known yet in England.

There were always plenty of meat dishes, roasted mutton, veal or beef, for instance, and besides these, roast chicken, or rabbit pie, roast goose, even boiled larks or sparrows. Can you remember what they grew for their salads? (see page 24). The gentry had white bread but the rest usually got brown. For drinks there was wine from France or Spain for the higher people and ale or cider for the lower ones. After several courses came the sweets which everyone liked. There was gingerbread and marchpane (made from pounded almonds, pistachio nuts, sugar and flour), tarts, marmalade and jellies. You can guess that dinner took a long time. William Harrison said that if anyone tried to taste every dish brought round he would make himself ill, but probably most people did not try. Perhaps it was to cool themselves after all this eating and drinking that in summer time Bess and her company would climb the stairs right up to the roof after dinner. They would walk along the roof ridge and take their dessert and wine in the south turret room, looking out over the green, rolling countryside which glowed in the afternoon sunlight.

In summer time after their long, elaborate dinner Elizabethan ladies and gentlemen liked to enjoy their gardens. The younger ones would play skittles or bowls in the shady bowling alley. Perhaps Bess and her older guests would sit in a bower scented with honeysuckle or roses, talking and sipping sweet wine and eating candied roses and marigolds. Or they might play cards. In bad weather there was the long gallery for strolling and talking. You could play *battledore and shuttlecock* there, or have a game of chess. Elizabethans were fond of asking riddles or playing a game of question and answer.

There were large numbers of servants in noble households. When the Earl of Derby was 'living quietly' in the country he had one hundred servants. Bess's household was fairly small – about thirty indoor servants. Why do you think people in those days were able to have so many servants? A man named John Harrington wrote a list of rules for servants. Here are some of them:

If absent from morning or evening meals or prayers, 2*d* fine.
Late for dinner, 2*d* fine.
Anyone going to the kitchen without reason, 1*d* fine.
For each oath, 1*d* fine.
For a dirty shirt on Sunday or a missing button, 6*d* fine.

A garden scene of about 1613. What are all the different people doing?

After 8 a.m. no bed must be found unmade or fireplace or candle box unclean.
Hall must be cleaned in one hour.
Guests' rooms must be cleaned within four hours of their departure.
The whole house must be swept and dusted every Friday.
Rising time 6 in winter, 5 in summer.

Some guests were not as particular as they ought to have been and it must have been a job to clear up after them. One guest room had this little verse (or posy, as they called it) painted on the wall:

With curtains some make *scabbards* clean, with coverlet their shoe:
All dirt and *mire*, some wallow in bed, as spaniels use to do.

Bess had many people working for her outside as well as inside. She had a steward to manage all her outside affairs. For a long time this was Timothy Pusey who was paid £10 a year. He kept good accounts which tell us how Bess's money came from farms and even from some coal mines and a glassworks. Under him was John Harrison, a clerk who kept household accounts from which we discover what Bess spent on food, wages and other things. She had seventeen bailiffs in charge of farms and among the outdoor servants at Hardwick were milkmaids, gardeners, millers, carpenters, saddlers, huntsmen and many others. Once a fortnight Bess would go through the accounts with Pusey or Harrison and sign them.

If she was inspecting her outdoor servants Bess might

find the gardeners busy sweeping the sanded paths that were kept so beautifully clean or trimming the little box edgings in the knot garden. Then she might pick some herbs or flowers from the garden needed to concoct a medicine. Some of her medicines sound rather nice: oil of roses for toothache, or a sweet paste made of rosebuds and sugar for stomach-ache. But another medicine, spiders swallowed whole in treacle, for fever, would not have been so pleasant.

Bess might also inspect some of the outbuildings at the back of the house. Here, beside the stables, were the *dovecote*, the mill and the smithy, the carpenter's shop, pigsties and chicken houses. Most of what was needed in the household was grown or made at home or on Bess's farms. She even had fishponds made and stocked them with pike, carp, perch and other fish. But the Clerk of the Kitchen sent to Hull, the nearest port, for luxuries like dried fruits, hops, salad oil, wine and figs.

Bess's servants had to work hard but she looked after them when they were ill and she was generous when they got married. For instance, Henry the Cook got an extra £5 on his marriage and also a fine supper party to which even the kitchen boy was invited. They had a merry time. The party cost 5*s.* 4*d.* (26½p) Even when she dismissed bad servants Bess was not mean. We find in her accounts that she gave a *tirewoman* £2 'at her going away, not for good service but for charity'.

Among Bess's servants were probably several musicians who played the lute, violin, flute, recorder and perhaps trumpet or cornet. The little band would play when the servants marched in with all the dishes for dinner and probably while Bess and her company were

Ladies and gentlemen making music together. Notice the lady playing the virginals

eating. Afterwards, in the long gallery, they could dance the slow, stately pavane or the quick, lively jig, or the volta in which you jumped as high as you could, while the little band played away like mad.

Both gentlemen and ladies went hunting and hawking. Bess and her husband would ride out with a lively party for a whole day's sport. Their huntsmen would have been up very early to discover where the deer were lurking in the woods. The ladies and gentlemen would wear their usual elaborate clothes. It must have been difficult to hunt in these. After the kill there would be a grand picnic in the woods.

Supper would be about 6 p.m., when everyone would eat the same kind of meal as at dinner, only rather less. There was no teatime, of course. People went to bed early because candle-light was not strong enough for reading or embroidery. As with getting up, there was quite a ceremony in going to bed. First, the servants of the bedchamber put a silver *warming pan* into their master or mistress's bed and lit the wax candle. They warmed a nightgown and night cap. It took some time to help their lord or lady out of all those heavy clothes. Bess or her husband might sit by the fire a little while in a dressing gown of, perhaps, black damask trimmed with fur and drink a *posset*. Then they would climb into the vast bed and sink into the feather mattress, while the servant drew the heavy curtain all round the bed to keep out draughts. As for the poor weary servant, he or she would pull out a little truckle bed from under the big one and sleep on that, while one little *rush-light* dimly lit the room.

The ladies and gentlemen who waited on Bess probably slept two or three together in one room, but the lower servants had to sleep just anywhere, in passages

A hunting picnic. Where is the food and drink?

and cupboards. Some of them actually had to go up to the roof to bed. They walked along the roof-ridge and down the sloping roof to the turret rooms on either side. Imagine what going to bed was like on a dark, cold, windy winter night! The Master Cook, however, was important enough to have his own room and a bed with a feather mattress.

6 *Festivities*

Winters were hard for poor people and even the rich in Elizabethan times were often cold and uncomfortable in those vast and draughty rooms with no central heating. So we need not be surprised that they cheered themselves up by a tremendous celebration at Christmas. 'Christmas comes but once a year', they said. 'And when it comes it bring good cheer.' The jollifications lasted for twelve days. I expect you know the carol 'The Twelve Days of Christmas'. Here is a verse from another carol written by someone at the time:

When Christmastide comes in like a bride
With Holly and Ivy *clad*,
Twelve Days in the year, much mirth and good cheer
In every household is had.

Beforehand Bess's farm people would be very busy killing birds and beasts for the feast. 'Now capon and hens, besides turkeys, geese and ducks, besides beef and mutton, must all die for the great feast', wrote one Elizabethan writer. Imagine the skinning and plucking, the chopping and seasoning, the boiling and roasting that went on in the great kitchen. On Christmas Eve the woodmen went into the woods to chop down the *Yule* log which they dragged home, decorated with holly and ivy, and brought in with music and dancing.

On Christmas Day the whole household, with guests and their servants, villagers and strangers, feasted in the great hall. There might be one hundred people altogether. We can picture the scene. At the high table Bess and her husband and children and guests sit with gleaming silver and gold dishes all laid out. In front of them stands a huge silver-gilt salt-cellar decorated with beautiful little figures. Down the long tables the servants, guest servants and any neighbours and strangers who come in will soon be sitting, all according to their rank. The Yule log blazes in the great fire-place while the firelight flickers on the bright reds and purples and blues of the tapestries, and on silver and gold.

The servants bring silver basins and napkins for the hand-washing at the high table. Then, with a flourish of trumpets, the great procession marches in with steaming dishes piled high. First come servants with torches and musicians playing, then the steward, treasurer and all the servers, carvers and ushers. They carry in front the *wassail cup*, wreathed with holly and ivy. The first and

A painting of about 1596 showing ladies and gentlemen at a wedding feast

greatest dish is a whole *boar's* head, roasted and decorated with rosemary and bayleaves, with a lemon placed between his gleaming teeth. The cook carrying the dish high chants the Boar's Head Carol:

The boar's head in hand I bear,
Bedecked with bays and rosemary;
And I pray you my masters be merry,
Quot estis in convivio.

The last line, which is in Latin, means 'All you at the feast'.

Soon everyone is busy devouring large amounts of food and drinking ale and mead from pewter tankards. The menu is wonderful. This is what they ate at one feast: 9 pieces of boiled and 6 pieces of roast beef, a haunch and leg of pork, 2 legs of veal, a young pig, a loin and breast of veal, 2 rabbits, 10 beef pasties, 2 mutton pasties, 4 venison pasties, 3 geese, 2 capons, 2 partridges, a woodcock, 12 larks. Sometimes there is a peacock roasted in his feathers. Sometimes great pies, 3 metres round, weighing 75 kilograms, are wheeled round on little carts; they are stuffed with geese, rabbits, ducks and pigeons. At the end of the feast they have sweets: marchpane gilded with gold, purple jellies, marmalade, tarts and almond biscuits.

When everyone is beginning to feel they cannot eat a bite more, they hear cheers and laughter at the screen's door and in come the *mummers*, disguised in animal heads or dressed as the characters in a play – St George, the Dragon, the Doctor and the heathen Slasher. A space is cleared and everyone laughs and claps as they do their comic play and dances. Someone wrote this little verse about the mummers:

Mummers who have just arrived. What characters do you think they are meant to represent?

To *mask* and to *mum* kind neighbours will come,
With wassails of nut brown ale;
To drink and *carouse* to all in this house,
As merry as *bucks* in the pale;
Where cake, bread and cheese is brought for your fees
To make you the longer stay.

The mummers have an earthenware Christmas box in which they collect money. At the end of their round they break the box and share out the cash. Afterwards everyone is ready to dance or play games such as blind man's buff. They go on feasting and dancing all through the next days. Many humble people from nearby villages get a good feed and strangers often come without being asked. On New Year's Day people give each other presents.

One way in which people liked to enjoy themselves at Christmastime was by choosing a leader called the Lord of Misrule. This is how an Elizabethan writer, Philip Stubbes, described what happened after the Lord of Misrule was chosen:

> This chooseth 20, 40, 60 or a 100 *lusty* lads to wait upon his lordly majesty. Then he *invests* his men with his liveries of yellow, green or some other light and *wanton* colour and as though they were not *gaudy* enough, they *bedeck* themselves with scarfs, ribbons and laces, hanged all over with gold rings. On their legs they hang many bells and they borrow rich handkerchiefs to wave from their pretty *Mopsies* and loving Bessies. Then they have their hobby horses, dragons and other antics, with pipes and drummers to strike up the devil's dance. Then march this *heathen* company towards the church, their pipes piping, their drummers thundering, their stumps dancing, their bells jingling, their handkerchiefs swinging about their heads. Then the foolish people, they look, they stare, they laugh. Then they dance round the church yard and go to their banqueting house where they feast and dance all day and all night.

Did Stubbes approve of these men, do you think?

On the Twelfth Day after Christmas a big cake was cut up and the man who got the bean in his slice of cake became King of the Bean and chose his Queen. Then they had the last big feast. That was the end of Christmas. The great thing was to have given good cheer to all your servants and neighbours and to also poor beggars. This is what is meant by 'open house'.

There were other country festivals all through the year. When Bess and her family were at Chatsworth or at Hardwick they would enjoy these. On *Shrove Tuesday* Bess might watch the villagers tossing pancakes and playing a very rough game of football all through the village. At Easter there was another mummer's play and a big feast. Thomas Tusser says: 'Then calf and lamb walk towards the kitchen and the pastry, and wild fowl and March rabbits run dead into the dish.'

May Day was a time for merriment because the winter was over. Beforehand Bess's servants would be busy clearing out the old smelly rushes from the floors in the house and bringing fresh, sweet-smelling rushes and flowers to spread instead. On the evening before May Day the country people trooped into the woods to cut a young tree for the maypole. They decorated it with flowers and had about 20 oxen to drag it home. Then it was planted in the middle of the village and they chose a Lord and Lady of the May. On May Day everyone danced round the maypole. The *morris dancers* came prancing along in their bright costumes, with bells jingling at their ankles and coloured ribbons and handkerchiefs fluttering. The hobby horse was galloping around, all dressed up with ribbons and bells, while special characters like Robin Hood, Maid Marian and Friar Tuck were all there. Besides the morris dancers everyone joined in jigs, hornpipes and other country dances. The musicians played away on violins, recorders, fife and drum until everyone was out of breath and threw themselves laughing on the ground.

On St John's Eve (23 June) we should see bonfires alight on hills round about, and fiery wheels being rolled down hill. Young men would jump through the fire and have wrestling and racing competitions. At Michaelmas (29 September) the household feasted on fat goose, and for *All Hallow E'en* Bess's baker made a special kind of

Morris dancers. Find the hobby horses. What other curious things can you see?

seed cake and the servants had fun in the great hall ducking for apples. Do you know how to play this?

Most of these were country festivities but Bess and her family sometimes had grander entertainments in the long gallery. The Northampton *waits* came to Hardwick once to play and sing and the Earl of Rutland's musicians gave a concert for Bess.

As the seasons went round Elizabethan people living in the country enjoyed many festivals. They ate and drank a lot at these times, but they also made their own music and were entertained by village players and dancers. People could be merry, even when life was hard, and England in the time of Elizabeth was often called Merry England.

7 *Living Dangerously*

In the sixteenth century important people at the royal Court lived dangerous lives because *Tudor* kings and queens liked their own way and were quickly angry with anyone who did not do just as they wanted. When Bess was a young woman there was the dangerous moment when Mary Tudor became Queen and tried to make everyone return to the Catholic Church. She was suspicious of Bess and her husband, Sir William Cavendish, because they had been on the Protestant side.

When the Protestant Elizabeth became Queen, Bess came back into favour again and in fact became one of the Queen's best friends. 'There is no lady in this land that I better love and like', Elizabeth once said. But, like the Queen herself, Bess enjoyed making schemes and she had to be very careful that her schemes did not interfere with Elizabeth's. Once she got caught out by getting mixed up in a plot for the secret marriage of one of the Queen's ladies-in-waiting. The Queen disapproved, and she was furious when she found out. Bess was put in prison in the Tower for some months as a punishment.

Bess learnt her lesson and after that was very careful to please the Queen. She and her husband always gave Elizabeth a gift on New Year's Day and Bess chose these carefully. In 1576 they gave her a special travelling outfit which included a cloak of peach-coloured satin embroidered with flowers and lined with spangled silk.

In fact the Queen must have trusted Bess and her fourth husband, George Talbot, Earl of Shrewsbury, a great deal, for when Mary Queen of Scot escaped to England in 1568 it was Talbot whom Elizabeth chose to guard her. You can read in another Then and There book, 'Mary Queen of Scots and the Scottish Reformation', why Mary came to England. For Elizabeth, Mary was a great problem: she wanted her treated like a queen, and yet she had to have her guarded like a prisoner because at once discontented Catholics started plots to make her queen of England, instead of Elizabeth. For the Earl of Shrewsbury Mary was also a great problem. He did not want to be her gaoler but he could not refuse the Queen's command. For the next sixteen years he was really tied down to the unpleasant job of keeping his prisoner safe.

His main problem was to make Mary comfortable in a place where she could be properly guarded. She was first taken to one of the Earl's castles at Tutbury, but the roof was leaky, the walls cracked and there was almost no furniture. Bess had a great rush to get everything ready in just two weeks. When Mary arrived, she found the place damp, gloomy and smelly, because the privies were bad. To the Earl's horror she brought sixty servants with her. He asked her to reduce them to thirty and wrote to the Queen's minister, Cecil, for £500 more to feed them all.

Tutbury was very inconvenient for a large number of people: there was not enough food, coal or hay, let alone rooms, for so many. So Mary was soon moved to another of the Earl's houses at South Wingfield where she could

Mary, Queen of Scots. Where is the date on this picture? Find out what the Latin (top left) means.

live in larger rooms. Poor Mary! She was never allowed to stay anywhere in comfort for long because people would begin plotting around her. So she would be hurried away from one place to a safer one. Being bundled backwards and forwards was not at all pleasant, for travelling was difficult and often very cold. For the Earl and Bess it was a real headache to arrange journeys for so many people and feed them. There were Mary's attendants, a band of soldiers to guard her and all the Earl's servants needed to look after them. This usually meant moving about 200 people, but several times about

400. Altogether, during the sixteen years in which he was her gaoler the Earl had to move Mary forty-six times! And he had to pay the expenses too. Queen Elizabeth allowed him £52 a week for Mary's keep but he spent much more and Elizabeth never really paid him properly. By the end the Earl had actually spent a great deal of his own fortune in guarding Mary for the Queen.

Although she made such trouble for them, Bess and her husband really tried to be kind to Mary. The Scots Queen (as people called her) liked Bess. The Earl wrote to Cecil: 'Mary goes daily to my wife's chamber where she sits devising works [doing embroidery]. Her talk is altogether of indifferent [unimportant] trifling matters, without any secret dealing, I assure you.' Can you think why he was so anxious for Cecil to know that they only gossiped about little things?

Bess and Mary both loved doing embroidery and Mary could show Bess many new designs. They worked mostly on small pieces which were later put together by Bess's embroiderers for hangings and curtains.

You can still see a piece of Mary's embroidery at Holyrood Palace outside Edinburgh. It has a cat sitting watching a mouse. Later on, another embroiderer gave the cat red hair and a crown. Can you guess who the cat and the mouse are meant to be?

At first, Mary's life with the Talbots was quite pleasant, although she knew she was a prisoner. But the plotters would not keep away and Mary could not stop herself from joining in their plots. Cecil grew more and more anxious and ordered the Earl to guard Mary more closely, cut down the number of her servants and stop all visitors. He even ordered the Earl to forbid Bess to see Mary. The poor Earl had a terrible time trying to treat

Hardwick embroidery showing a family scene. What are they all doing? Find the windmill and the castle

Mary as kindly as he could but not let Cecil and the Queen think that he was favouring her too much. He had to watch closely to catch the plotters and get hold of letters passing between them and Mary. He was losing money all the time. At last the anxiety about Mary began to make George Talbot irritable and cross. He could not see his friends, or go to London when he wished; he could not even see Bess unless she came to him. And it was at this time that he began to quarrel with his wife.

Finally the Queen gave way and found another gaoler for Mary in 1584, but even then the Earl of Shrewsbury had not seen the last of her, for he had the terrible task of being a witness when she was executed in 1587.

By then Bess must have known very well that it was dangerous to do anything that went against Queen Elizabeth's plans. But she had great hopes for the grand future of her family and so she wanted them to marry as high up as possible. In 1574 she arranged a marriage between her youngest daughter, Elizabeth, and Charles Stuart, Earl of Lennox. This was a dangerous thing to do because Charles belonged not only to the Scottish royal family but also to a branch of the Tudor royal house in England. So he might try to claim the English throne. But he died quite soon leaving his wife with one daughter, Arabella, who was, of course, Bess's grand-daughter. Queen Elizabeth was very angry over this marriage, for she hated anyone to start planning about her successor and always suspected a plot to turn her off the throne. She put Charles Stuart's mother in the Tower for a few months, but it looks as if Bess was luckier. She took good care to tell the Queen how loyal she was and to give her good presents. In fact, as you know, the Queen liked Bess, so she did not put her out of favour.

Bess adored her grandchild Arabella. Although she lived away in the country with her grandmother, Arabella was educated to go to Court. She learnt to speak French and Italian, to play on the lute and to

Arabella Stuart aged about fourteen. How many animals and birds has she?

dance the Court dances. In 1587, when she was 12, she was allowed to pay a visit to Court for the Queen to inspect her. Bess had spoilt Arabella and she disgraced herself at Court by giving herself too many airs and was sent home. The tutors who taught her must have found her a tiresome child. Once Bess's steward wrote to his mistress when she was away: 'My Lady Arbella at 8 o'clock this evening was merry, and eats her meat well: but she went not to school these 6 days, therefore I would be glad of your ladyship's coming.' It needed Bess to manage her granddaughter, and I don't think she would stop at whipping her if necessary. Poor Arabella! All her life she wanted to be a princess and then a queen, but she never was. All the same, Bess worked very hard for her children and helped to make their families some of the most powerful in England.

8 The End

When she was an old lady Bess lived mostly at Hardwick. But she never gave up her liking for building and furnishing new houses and quite late in life was building a cosy little one at Owlcotes (home for owls), 3 miles from Hardwick. Apart from this her chief interest was in Arabella and her plans for marrying her to someone important.

Bess had spent a lifetime on building houses and building up her family as well, but she also gave some thought to God and you would have found her at church on every Sunday. Over the mantel of her low great chamber at Hardwick she had these words carved: 'The *conclusion* of all things is to feare God and keepe his

commandementes'. Bess died in 1608. She had made a careful will, leaving most of her property to her children and grand-children. But she left £1,000 to her servants and money to buy them *mourning rings*. Arabella got £1,000 and also a crystal glass cup, set with precious stones, and Bess's *sable* and pearls. A splendid tomb was built in Derby Church to the memory of a grand lady.

The Hardwick Coat of Arms over the fireplace in the Withdrawing Room. The Latin words mean: The stag, noble in blood, horn, heart, eye, foot and ear, and made more noble by the fame of its burden

How Do We Know?

There were many other Elizabethans building beautiful new houses in England at this time. Although some of these houses, like Chatsworth, were pulled down later to build grander ones, many are still standing, sometimes with the furniture, tapestries, pictures and other things their owners collected still in them. Bess's house at Hardwick holds many of her possessions. When you walk round these houses probably your first thought will be: what large rooms, what elaborate decorations, and what big gardens and parks they had!

In those days there were plenty of workers to build and servants to clean these large places. Today very few people can afford to live like the Elizabethan ladies and gentlemen. So many families who own Elizabethan houses now may open their houses for people to come and see, and try to charge enough to meet their expenses. Or they may hand over their houses to the National Trust, an organisation which looks after fine houses and beautiful parts of the countryside. The National Trust opens these houses to visitors so we can see them for ourselves. If you are a member you get free entrance to all National Trust properties. For joining, and to find out about the special subscription for young people or belonging as a family, write to The National Trust, Membership Department, P.O. Box 30, Beckenham, Kent, BR3 4TL.

Bess kept accounts and she wrote and received many letters. Most of these are now at Chatsworth. The accounts tell us much about what she and her family bought, what they ate, how many servants they had and what they paid them, as well as how much their buildings cost. The inventory Bess made in 1601 tells us exactly how she furnished her house at Hardwick. This is what she had in the 'Best Bed Chamber':

> Fyve peeces of hanginges of grene velvett and cloth of gold and silver set with trees, with long borders of stories in nedleworke, everie peece being Eight foote deep, a bedsted, the postes being covered with black velvet and layde with three layers of golde and silver lace, a tester, bedes head and vallans of black velvett, imbrodered with nedleworke flowers, fringed with golde, blewe and grene silk frenge, fyve guilt knobs to stand on top of the bed, fyve Curtins of Changeable damask, a mattress, a fetherbed, too pillowes, too blankets, a quilt of india stuff imbrodered with beastes with frenge and tassells of white silk, a square table, a Carpet for it of cloth of silver and purple velvett frenged with yellowe and blewe silk, a Cubberd guilt and inlayde, a Carpet for it of blewe velvett imbrodered with nedleworke flowers with black and yellowe silk frenge, a Chare of cloth of silver and grene with yellowe silk frenge, a stoole of cloth of gold and grene velvett, layde with silver lace and silver frenge, too quitions [cushions] of cloth of gold lyned with yellowe sattin stript with silver and with tassells of golde, purple and red silke, a fyer shovell, a payre of tonges.

And here you can picture to yourself the grand decorations in the gallery:

> Thirtene peeces of deep Tapestrie hanginges of the storie of Gedeon, everie peece being nyntene foote deep, too square inlayde tables, too fayre turkie Carpets for them, too other needlework Carpets, one with my Ladies Armes in the middest with a deep gold frenge and lyned with red sarcenet, a chare of nedleworke with gold and silver lace and silver and crimson silk frenge, an other chare of nedleworke with yellowe and blewe silk frenge, a foot stoole of velvet, a lowe stoole of black and grene velvett and cloth of golde with goldelace and with golde and silver frenge, a lowe stoole of nedleworke with blewe and white

> silk frenge, a forme covered with crimson and white damask with yellow and grene silk frenge, nyntene long quitions: one for the Chare the ground purple velvett imbrodered with gold and silver with beastes, birds and flowers, with silver and black silk frenge, oring [orange] tawnie silk and silver tassells; the rest for the windowes: too long quitions of Crimson satin imbroidered with Straweberries and wormes with blewe silk frenge and tassells, an other with flowers, straweberries and oke leaves, frenge and tassells of grene silk and silver, an other long quition of hunting the hare, an other long quition of Chatesworth house with greene, red and yellow silk frenge, buttons of Carnation silke and silver [and thirteen more 'quitions'].

Letters tell us more about people's feelings: how they fell in love, or got angry, how they made plans and sometimes got into desperate difficulties.

Many Elizabethan writers have described the kind of life they lived. Those little conversations about children in Chapter 2 were written by a schoolmaster who was teaching English to French people. Thomas Tusser wrote about what good farmers and their wives ought to do and so he shows us a good deal of country life. Philip Stubbes wrote about things he disliked, such as ridiculous clothes and the wild revels of the Lord of Misrule. John Harrison wrote a description of England and several people made books of recipes for food or medicines. Shakespeare brought country people into some of his plays, and there are other writers who tell us about their gardens and games, their music and dancing and feasts. So, from their things and their pictures and what they wrote, we can find out enough to imagine these Elizabethan people at home in their large draughty houses.

Things to Do

1. Write a conversation between either the boys and their tutor or the girls and their mistress after their mother had gone (see pages 17 and 20).
2. Hold a discussion in class about the differences between the education of Elizabethan children and our own.
3. Find out if there is an Elizabethan house near you and, if so, try to visit it. Draw a plan of the main rooms.
4. If you can visit Hardwick Hall itself, make drawings of it and of Elizabethan things there and start a book about the Elizabethan Country House in which you can gather all kinds of pictures. Or you could do the same with another Elizabethan house near you.
5. Visit a museum to study and draw Elizabethan costume, furniture, musical instruments etc.
6. Draw pictures of a man and a woman in Elizabethan dress, or you could make puppets and dress them.
7. Imagine you are one of Bess's servants. Describe where you work and write an account of all you do in one day.
8. Find out about the flowers and fruits in an Elizabethan garden and draw pictures of them.
9. Make an Elizabethan frieze to go round the classroom. You could include mummers and musicians and all sorts of people.
10. Study the pieces of Bess's inventory on pages 72–3 and puzzle out the queer spelling. Then write out the list in modern spelling and illustrate it with pictures.
11. Listen to some Elizabethan songs on records and if you are learning to play an instrument or sing, try one or two of them for yourselves.

12. Get up an Elizabethan country festival for yourselves (e.g. Christmas, Twelfth Night, May Day). You could dress up as mummers or morris dancers.
13. Hold a class debate on whether you would rather live in an Elizabethan country house or in a modern one.

Glossary

alabaster, marble
All Hallow E'en, evening before All Saints' Day (November 1st)
astronomy, study of the stars
banquet, feast
battledore and shuttlecock, game rather like badminton
bear-baiting, sport in which a captive bear is attacked by dogs
to bedeck, to decorate
birch, here means a bunch of twigs used for whipping children
boar, fierce wild pig
bodice, tight-fitting top part of a woman's dress
buck, male deer
buffet, here means sideboard
buttery, place where drinks are made and kept
to carouse, to drink and be merry
catch, here means a tune to sing
Catholic, here means the Church Henry VIII rejected, but set up again by Mary, and rejected once more by Elizabeth
chamber, room
changeable, here means the colour blue
chemise, woman's underwear
clad, clothed
conclusion, final result
coronet, small crown
cut-work, a kind of embroidery
damask, rich cloth with patterns woven in it
diligent, hard-working
to doff, to take off

doth, old word for does
doublet, Elizabethan jacket for men
dovecote, house for doves
dowry, money or property given to a daughter usually at marriage
ewry, room where ewers (jugs for water) are kept
falconer, man who looks after falcons (birds of prey) trained for sport
farthingale, wheel-shaped frame of wire to hold out ladies' skirts
to fence, mock fight with swords
frieze, a long decoration on a wall
gaudy, brightly coloured
gilded, covered with gold
good morrow, good morning
hath, old word for *has*
heathen, someone without Christian beliefs
horn-book, wooden bat, with alphabets and letters on it, covered with horn
hose, stockings
ink-horn, container for ink
inventory, list of furniture etc.
to invest, here means to dress people in special clothes
knot-garden, flower beds and paths made in a special pattern
litter, covered chair on poles in which ladies were carried round town
livery, uniform
lusty, vigorous and strong
lute, early musical instrument like a guitar
madrigal, song
manchet, white bread
to mask, to act plays (*masques*) disguised by false heads or masks
medlar, tree with brown fruit
minstrel, man who entertains by singing and playing
mire, mud
moat, ditch full of water round a castle
Mopsy, a girl's name

morris dancers, people decorated with bells and ribbons who do old dances
mourning ring, special ring given at a funeral
muckinder, a baby's bib
mummers, actors who *mum* (act) old plays
musk, a perfume
overmantel, decoration over a fireplace
overseer, person in charge of work
parlour, sitting-room (from French *parler*, to talk)
perplexity, being very puzzled
pomander, ball of scent to keep away smells
posset, drink made of hot milk and wine
privy, lavatory
Protestant, belonging to one of the new churches in the sixteenth century
quill, feather, used for a pen
quince, fruit rather like a pear
rush-light, rush dipped in grease and lighted as a candle
russet, reddish-brown
sable, rich brown fur
sarsenet, fine silk
scabbard, case for a sword
servery, room from which meals are served
Shrove Tuesday, day before Ash Wednesday when Lent begins
sluggish, lazy
spicery, place where spices are kept
sturgeon, kind of large fish
swaddling bands, strips of cloth wrapped round a small baby
taffeta, thin silk
tapestry, cloth with stories or patterns on it which have been either woven or embroidered in needlework
tawny, yellow brown
tester, cloth ceiling over a four-poster bed
tirewoman, lady's maid
Tudor, describing the time between the reigns of Henry VII and Elizabeth I
turkey carpet, carpet brought from Turkey, usually put on tables
turret, little tower sticking up above the roof

tutor, teacher for one or two children
usher, servant who announced people and arranged processions
valance, frill round a bed
venison, the meat from a deer
viola da gamba, an early stringed instrument like a 'cello
virginals, an early kind of keyboard instrument
waits, band of singers or actors
wanton, frivolous
warming-pan, pan filled with hot coals put in a bed to warm it
wassail cup, large cup or bowl of hot spiced wine handed round to drink
withdrawing room, room into which people went (withdrew) after dinner
yeoman, here means a servant in charge of a particular bit of the house (e.g. yeoman of the cellar)
Yule, old word for Christmas

Index